IMO OLYMPIAD WORKBOOK

1

SOF INTERNATIONAL MATHEMATICS OLYMPIAD 2023-24

SANAGE EDITORIAL BOARD

SANAGE
PUBLISHING HOUSE

Paperback: 978-811937372-7

Any references to historical events, real people, or real places are used fictitiously. Names, characters, and places are products of the author's imagination.

Printed by:

Sanage Publishing House LLP
Mumbai, India

sanagepublishing@gmail.com

Contents

CHAPTER 1

NUMBER SENSE

TOPICS COVERED:

* Identify numbers and their name upto 100
* What comes before, after and in between the numbers
* Compare numbers
* Identify numbers and their names using worksheet and place values
* Arrange numbers using ascending or descending order
* Skip counting
* Expanded form
* Count and write the number of given objects

MATHEMATICAL REASONING

1. **Which number will come in place of (?)?**

   A) Fifty Seven

   B) Fifty six

   C) Fifty eight

   D) Fifty five

2. **The expanded form of 78 is.**

   A) 7 + 60   B) 70 + 8   C) 7 + 8   D) 7 – 8

3. **Scale __________ shows the smallest number.**

   A) Q   B) S   C) R   D) P

4. **There are 5 ones and 6 tens in __________.**

   A) 56   B) 39   C) 42   D) 65

5. **Which of the following is an incorrect match ?**

6. **Which of the following is arranged in ascending order?**

7. **Which of the following pencil holder shows the number of given oranges?**

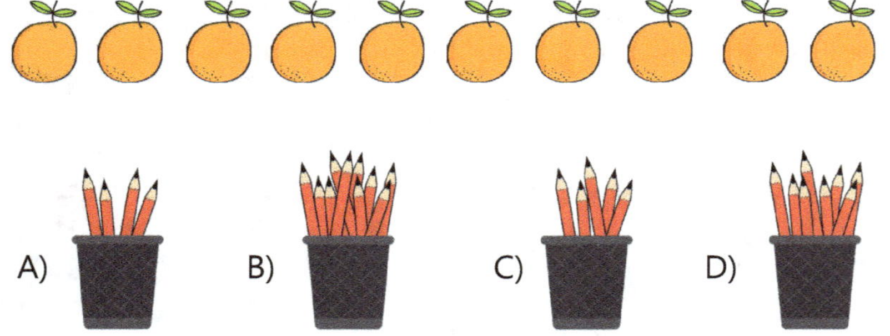

8. **What comes before 77 but after 75?**

A) 78   B) 76   C) 80   D) 74

9. **Which of the following is not on the writting pad?**

A) Sixty two   C) Ninety one

B) Seventy three   D) Thirty six

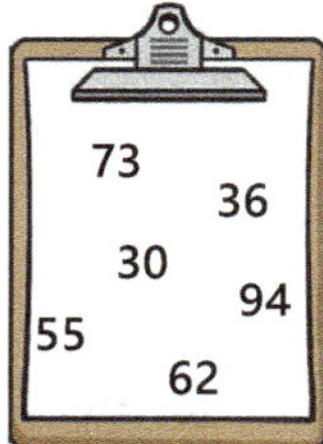

10. **The number on the given worksheet is _____________.**

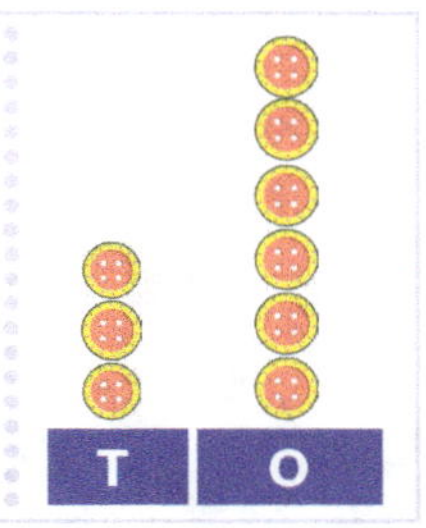

A) 5 tens 6 ones

B) 4 tens 7ones

C) 5 tens 8 ones

D) 3 tens 6 ones

11. **The given ruler line shows _____________.**

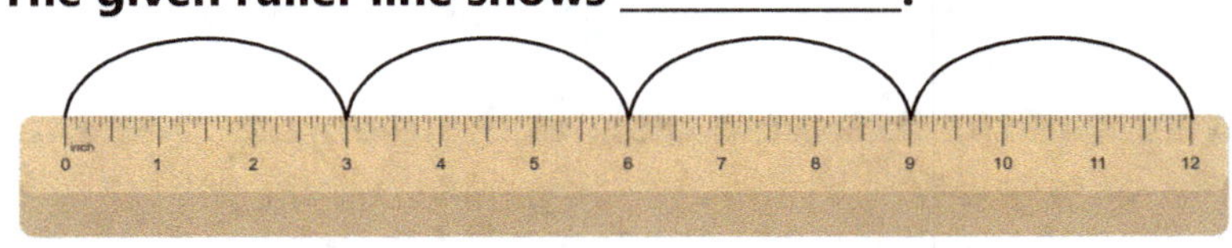

A) Counting by 1's   B) Counting by 3's

C) Counting by 5's   D) Counting by2's

12. **Which of the following jar has the highest number of candies?**

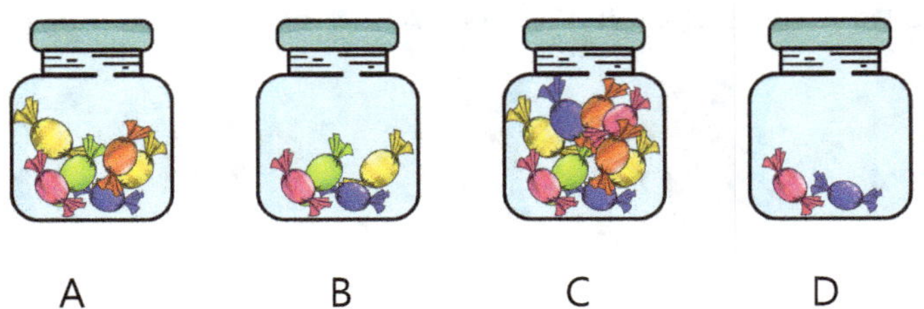

A   B   C   D

13. **Select correct match.**

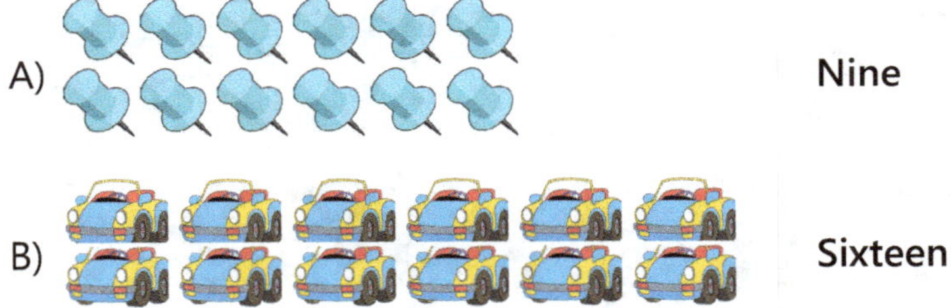

A)   Nine

B)   Sixteen

14. Which of the following sets has more objects than the given set of erasers?

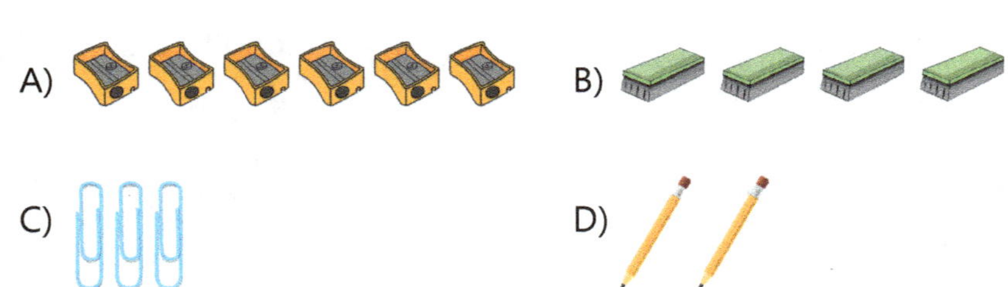

15. Five numbers are written on the five mangoes as follows.

Which mango shows the number lying between 31 and 41 and also having 4 at ones place?

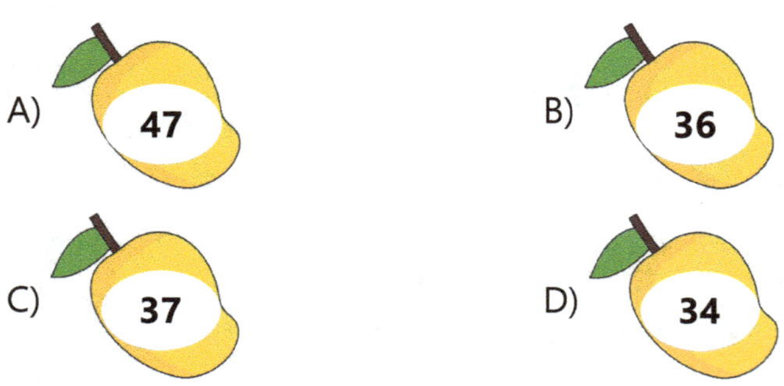

16. **Which basket has apples more than 2 but less than 5?**

A) B) C) D)

17. **Monica has following eraser and sharpeners.**

Which statement is false?

A) Erasers are more than sharpners.

B) Sharpners are less than erasers.

C) Sharpners are equal to erasers.

D) There are 4 erasers.

18. **How many butterflies are there in the given picture?**

A) 9 B) 5 C) 7 D) 11

19. **There are ______________ carrots in the given figure.**

A) Five B) Nine C) Twelve D) Ten

20. **Who has maximum number of candies?**

Neha	Rahul	Om	Jay

A) Om   B) Jay   C) Rahul   D) Neha

ACHIEVERS SECTION (HOTS)

21. **Select the correct option.**

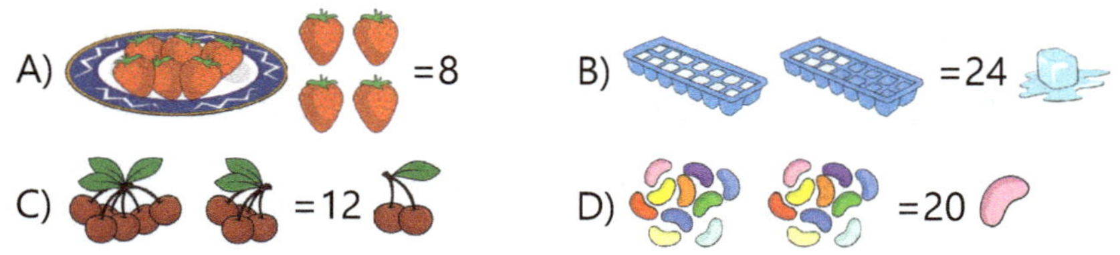

A) = 8   B) = 24

C) = 12   D) = 20

22. **Select the correct words from below numbered column.**

P   Q   R   S   T

Cone (1) is before cone Q. Cone (2) is after the cone S. Cone R is in (3) the cone Q and the cone S. Cone S is (4) the cone T.

	1	2	3	4
A)	P	T	between	after
B)	P	T	between	before
C)	P	R	after	after
D)	R	T	before	before

23. **Arrange the following in decending order.**

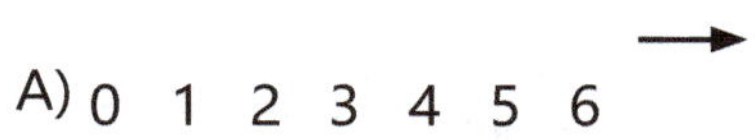 P.   3 tens 5 ones   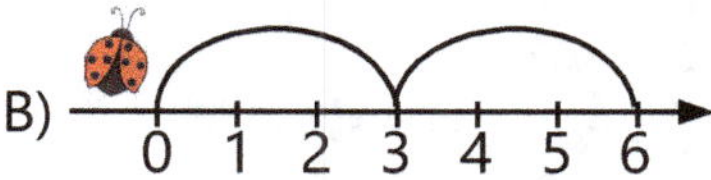 Q.   1 tens 3 ones

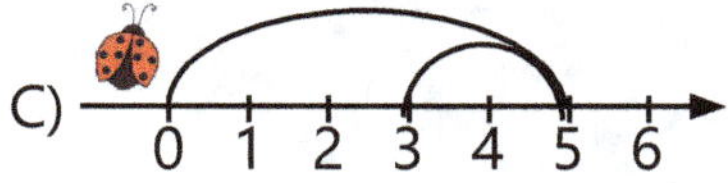 R.   2 tens 6 ones   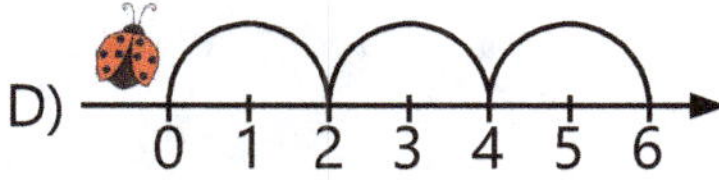 S.   5 tens 1 ones

A) P, R, S, Q   B) R, S, P, Q

C) Q, S, P, R   D) S, P, R, Q

24. **Which number line shows flight of lady bug by 2's?**

A) 0 1 2 3 4 5 6

B) 0 1 2 3 4 5 6

C) 0 1 2 3 4 5 6

D) 0 1 2 3 4 5 6

25. **Which worksheet shows the number comes before 27?**

A) 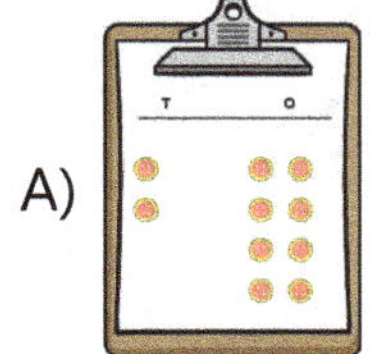   B) 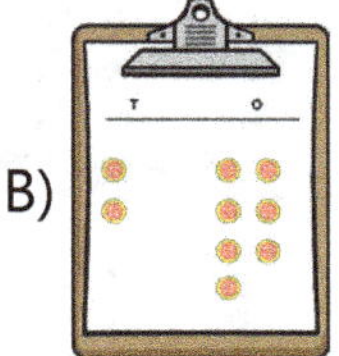   C) 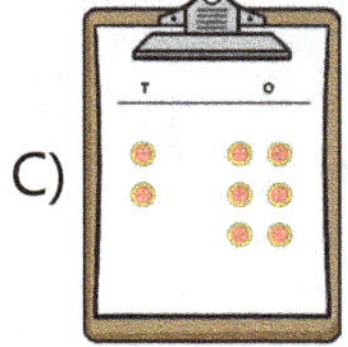   D) 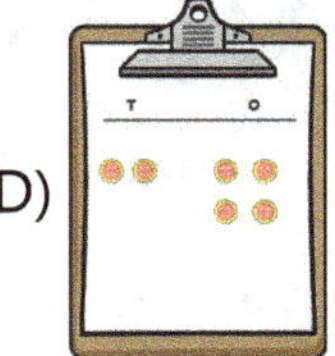

Colour your choice with color pencil				
1	**2**	**3**	**4**	**5**
A B C D	A B C D	A B C D	A B C D	A B C D
6	**7**	**8**	**9**	**10**
A B C D	A B C D	A B C D	A B C D	A B C D
11	**12**	**13**	**14**	**15**
A B C D	A B C D	A B C D	A B C D	A B C D
16	**17**	**18**	**19**	**20**
A B C D	A B C D	A B C D	A B C D	A B C D
21	**22**	**23**	**24**	**25**
A B C D	A B C D	A B C D	A B C D	A B C D

ADDITION

* Adding one digit and two digit in numbers
* Adding numbers given in form of number names and place values
* Addition on number line
* Solve word problem on addition
* Properties of 'zero' in addition

MATHEMATICAL REASONING

1. **Arrange the numbers on the leaf from the smallest to the greatest.**

20+2	10+4	7+5	11+9
P	Q	R	S

A) P, S, R, Q B) S, R, Q, P

C) Q, S, R, P D) R, Q, S, P

2. 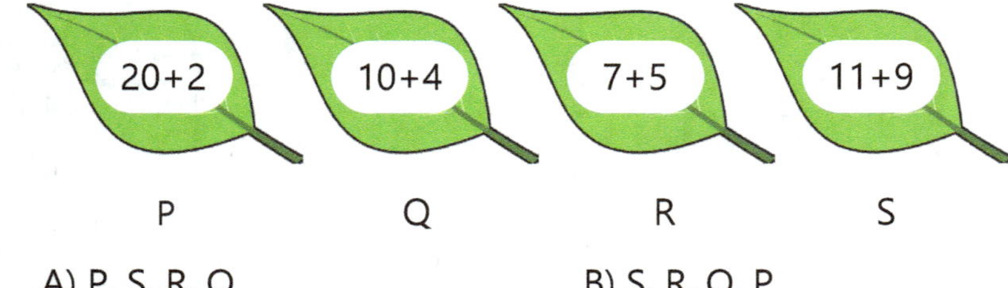 **shows**

A) 52 + 13 = 65 B) 74 + 11 = 85

C) 71 + 13 = 84 D) 70 + 8 = 78

3. **If Sneha add a number to 28, she will get 28. What number is she adding?**

$$20 + \boxed{} = 28$$

A) 2   B) 8   C) 28   D) 12

4. **Which of the following options will complete the given number bond?**

A) 3 tens + 5 ones

B) 3 tens + 2 tens

C) 3 tens + 2 ones

D) 2 tens + 3 ones

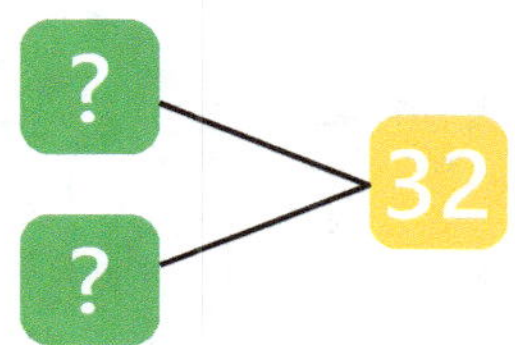

5. **Which of the following options shows the total number of pencils in both the pencil boxes?**

A) 6 + 4 = 10

B) 5 + 6 = 11

C) 7 + 8 = 15

D) 5 + 2 = 7

Pencil Box P

Pencil Box Q

6. **How much money is saved in the piggy bank given below?**

A) 60   B) 69   C) 62   D) 66

7. **Find the sum of two smallest numbers in the glass jar.**

A) 12   B) 21

C) 29   D) 22

8. **A frog jumps 2 setps from 0 and then 3 steps. Where will he reach?**

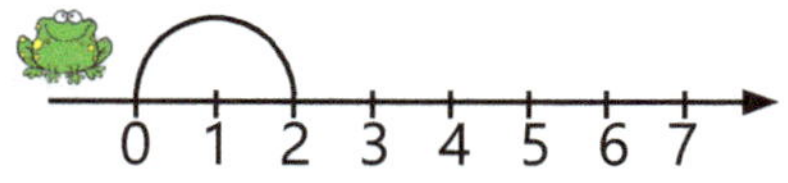

A) 5th Point   B) 4th point   C) 6th Point   D) 7th point

9. **21+3 is shown by which writing pad?**

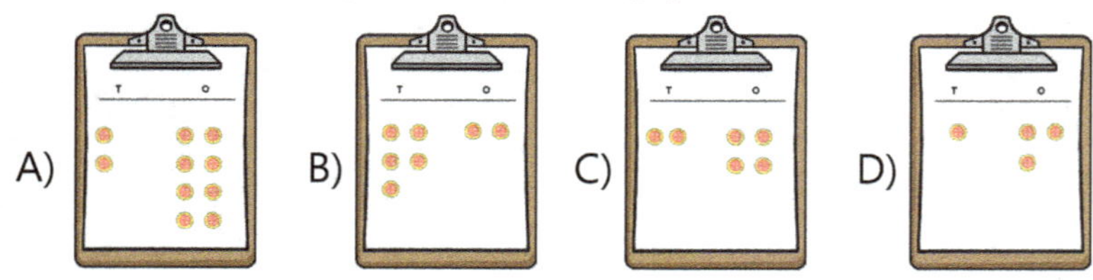

10. **Add the numbers on the given writing pads.**

A) 86

B) 76

C) 77

D) 80

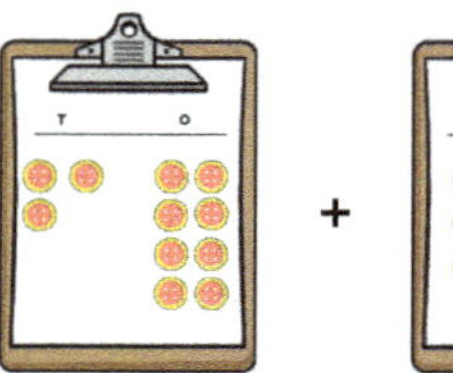

11. **Find the missing number.**

$$? + 4 = 15$$

A) 10   B) 11   C) 8   D) 12

DIRECTION (12-13): Study the given sets and answer the following questions.

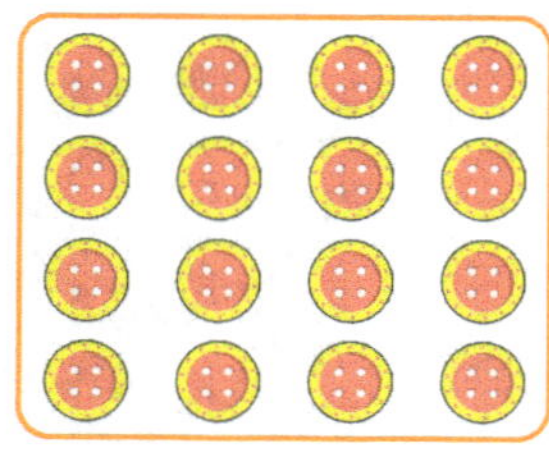

X

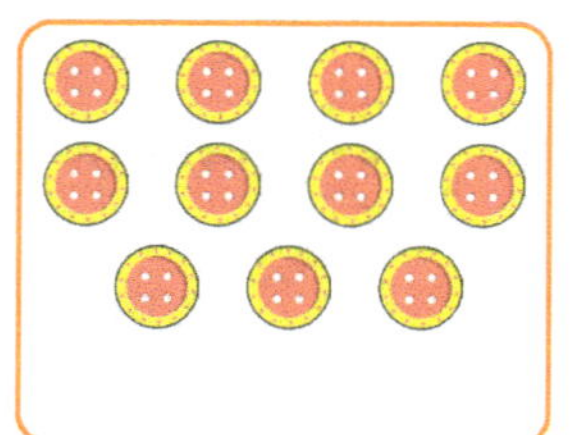

Y

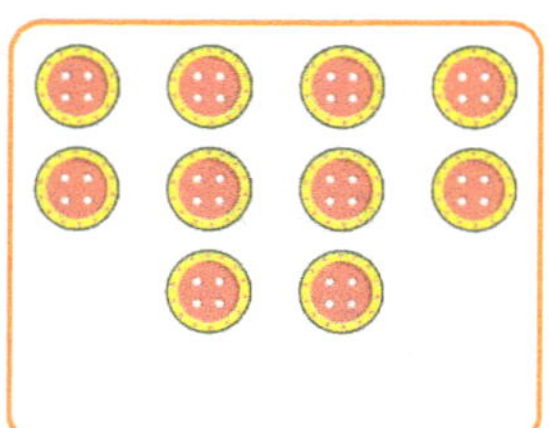

Z

12. **Find the total number of buttons in set Y and set Z.**

    A) 20   B) 21   C) 25   D) 15

13. **Find the total number of buttons in set X and set Z.**

    A) 26   B) 36   C) 29   D) 46

14. **Select the CORRECT option.**

    A) 32 + 22 = 52   B) 48 + 20 = 60

    C) 65 + 10 = 75   D) 35 + 23 = 55

15. **Which of the following options gives the answer smaller than 65?**

    A) 42 + 26   B) 58 + 20

    C) 35 + 30   D) 25 + 22

EVERYDAY MATHEMATICS

16. **In a garden, there are only 3 butterflies, 8 honey bees and 10 ladybugs. How many insects are there in the garden?**

    A) 20   B) 23   C) 19   D) 21

17. **Sonali has 23 candies. She buys 6 more candies. How many candies does she have altogether?**

    A) 22   B) 30   C) 29   D) 49

18. **There are 12 ladybugs and 22 honey bees in the garden. How many total number of insects are there in the garden?**

    A) 34   B) 44   C) 35   D) 42

19. There are only 

and ![birds] in the garden. How many total birds are there in the garden?

A) 12   B) 10   C) 6   D) 8

20. Sunil bought 15 chocolates on Monday, 8 chocolates on Tuesday and 25 chocolates on Wednesday. How many chocolates did he buy altogether?

A) 42   B) 40   C) 48   D) 28

ACHIEVERS SECTION (HOTS)

21. Sakshi and his 4 friends equally shared 20 chocolates. Each child received __ chocolates.

A) 10   B) 8

C) 5   D) 4

22. Find the value of P and Q respectively.

A) 1, 4   B) 2, 5

C) 2, 2   D) 1, 3

$$\begin{array}{r} P\;1 \\ +\;2\;4 \\ \hline 4\;Q \end{array}$$

23. 5 more than 10 is represented by which number line?

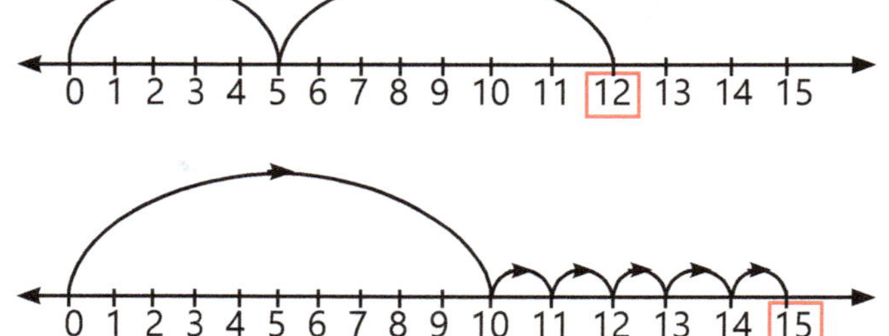

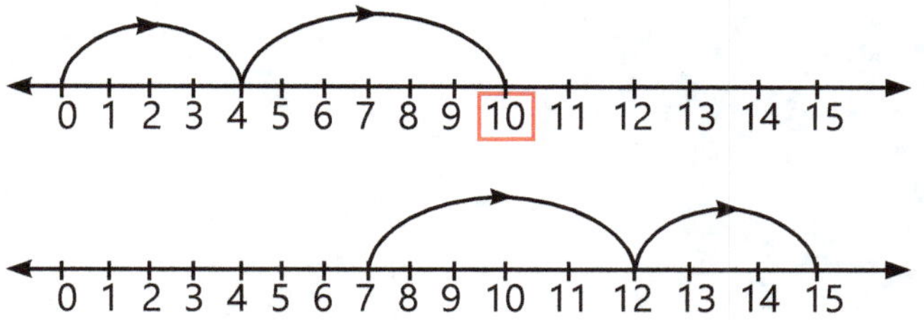

24. Which of the following options is INCORRECT?

A) 2 tens + 3 ones = 23

B) 2 tens + 3 ones = 22

C) 12 ones + 3 ones = 15

D) 20 ones + 5 ones = 25

25. Suresh has different types of sweets. He has 2 more jalebis than gulab jamuns. He has 5 more gulab jamuns than ladoos. If he has 2 ladoos, then the total number of sweets he has, is

A) 10　　　　B) 18　　　　C) 20　　　　D) 9

Colour your choice with color pencil				
1	**2**	**3**	**4**	**5**
A B C D	A B C D	A B C D	A B C D	A B C D
6	**7**	**8**	**9**	**10**
A B C D	A B C D	A B C D	A B C D	A B C D
11	**12**	**13**	**14**	**15**
A B C D	A B C D	A B C D	A B C D	A B C D
16	**17**	**18**	**19**	**20**
A B C D	A B C D	A B C D	A B C D	A B C D
21	**22**	**23**	**24**	**25**
A B C D	A B C D	A B C D	A B C D	A B C D

CHAPTER 3

SUBTRACTION

* Subtract by taking away
* Subtract one digit and two digit numbers
* Subtract numbers given in the form of number names and place values
* Subtraction on number line
* Solve word problems and subtraction

MATHEMATICAL REASONING

1. 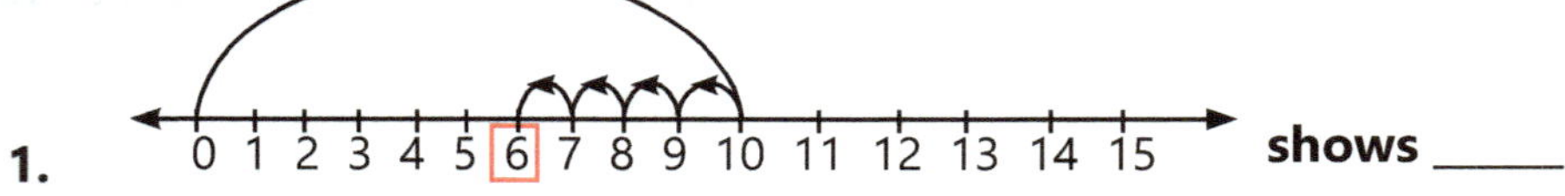 shows ______

A) 10 - 6 = 4   B) 8 - 6 = 2   C) 10 - 4 = 6   D) 10 + 6 = 16

2. **Which of the following number sentences represents the given picture?**

A) 20 - 5 = 15   B) 20 - 6 = 14   C) 15 - 9 = 6   D) 20 - 10 = 10

3. $\boxed{4 \text{ tens } 5 \text{ ones}} - \boxed{2 \text{ tens } 2 \text{ ones}} =$

A) 23   B) 15   C) 12   D) 15

4. **Which writing pad shows 28 – 10 = 18**

A) 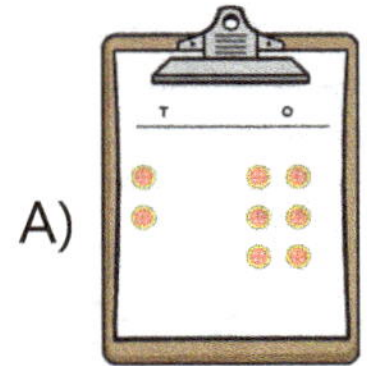 B) 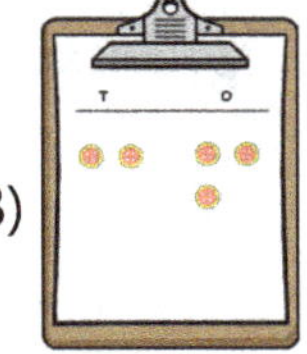 C) 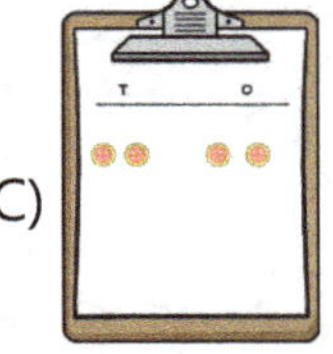 D) 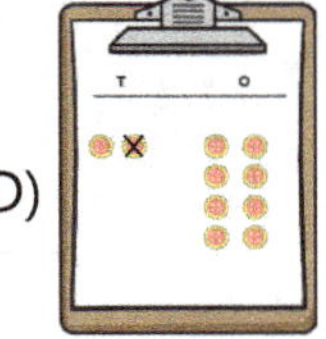

5. **The difference between the largest and the smallest number shown on the monitor is___________.**

A) 54   B) 74

C) 78   D) 38

6. **Which of the following is the CORRECT way of writing 4 less than 12?**

A) 12 - 4 = 8   B) 8 - 4 = 4   C) 12 - 8 = 4   D) 12 + 4 = 16

7. **How many buttons should be crossed (X) to show 6 buttons uncrossed?**

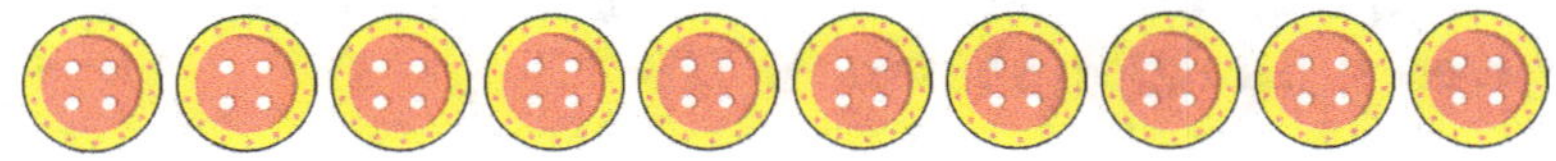

A) 10   B) 4   C) 8   D) 6

8. 

A) 18   B) 38   C) 28   D) 56

9. **Choose the CORRECT subtraction sentence for the given picture.**

A) 2 tens 6 ones - 3 ones   B) 6 tens 2 ones - 4 ones

C) 2 tens 8 ones - 6 ones   D) 2 tens 5 ones - 3 ones

10. **Which of the following number lines shows "8 - 3 = 5"?**

A) 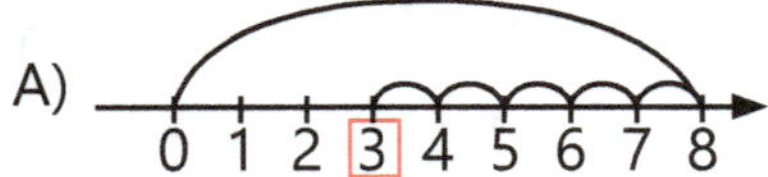

B) 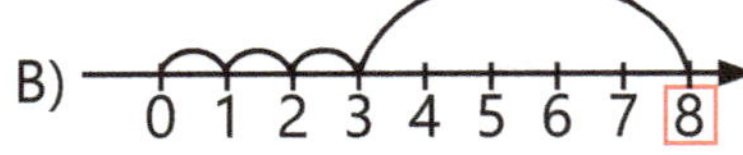

C) 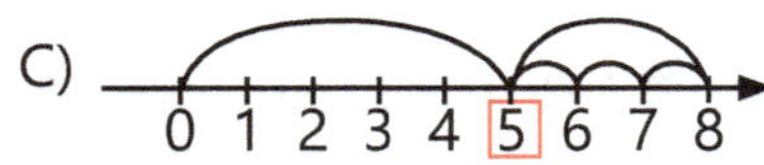

D) 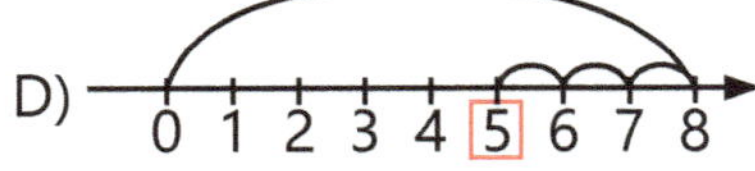

11. 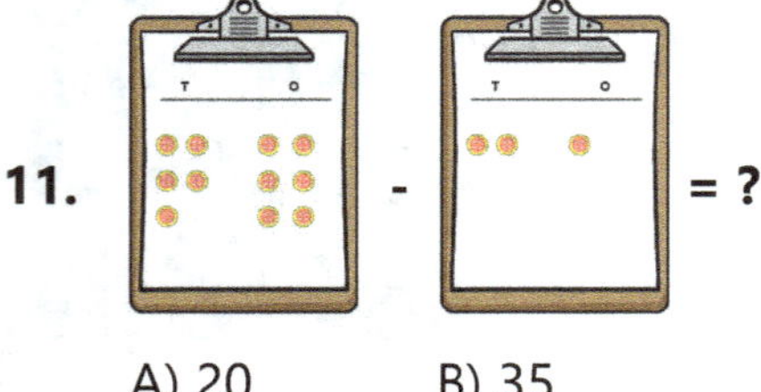 **- = ?**

A) 20   B) 35   C) 25   D) 21

12. **Which of the following options is CORRECT?**

A) 87 - 24 = 60   B) 38 - 15 = 22

C) 83 - 25 = 58   D) 74 - 32 = 40

13. **How many more candies should be crossed (X) to show the given subtraction sentence? "18 - 6"**

A) 2   B) 3   C) 5   D) 1

14. **Which of the following has the value more than "24"?**

A) 32 ones – 10 ones

B) 5 tens 2 ones – 2 tens

C) 2 tens 8 ones – 7 ones

D) 5 tens 8 ones – 4 tens 3 ones

15. **Which subtraction sentence gives same value as 53 - 22 ?**

A) 40 - 22   B) 48 - 17

C) $\boxed{37}$ - $\boxed{20}$ D) $\boxed{28}$ - $\boxed{21}$

EVERYDAY MATHEMATICS

16. **Anuj bought 45 chocolates. She gave 15 chocolates to her sister. How many chocolates are left with him?**

    A) 25   B) 35   C) 20   D) 30

17. **Riya has** (strawberries) **and** (cherries) **How many more cherries are needed so that cherries are equal to strawberries?**

    A) 7   B) 5   C) 8   D) 6

18. **There are** (ducks) **ducks in a pond.** (ducks) **ducks came out. Which number sentence represents the number of ducks left in the pond?**

    A) 6 - 3 = 4   B) 6 - 3 = 3   C) 6 - 3 = 2   D) 6 - 3 = 5

19. **Akshita ate 4** (candy) **chocolates from a box of 15** (candy) **chocolates. How many** (candy) **are left in the box?**

    A) 8   B) 9   C) 10   D) 11

20. **Sonal has 80 sweets. She gave 15 sweets to Neha and 25 sweets to Tina. How many sweets are left with her ?**

    A) 40   B) 50   C) 30   D) 20

ACHIEVERS SECTION (HOTS)

X	Y
-6	2
2	5

21. **Find the value of X and Y respectively.**

    A) 8, 6   B) 8, 7   C) 6, 8   D) 7, 8

22. **Match the following.**

Column 1   Column 2

1.   a.   9 - 3

2.   b.   7 - 2

3.   c.   8 - 4

4.   d.   6 - 3

A) (l) → (a), (2)→ (d), (3) → (c), (4) → (b)

B) (l)→ (c), (2)→ (d). (3)→ (b), (4)→ (a)

C) (!) → (b), (2) → (c). (3)→ (d), (4)→ (a)

D) (l)→ (c), (2)→ (d). (3)→ (a), (4)→ (b)

23. **If**   **= 20 and**   **= 10, then which of the following is correct?**

A)

B)

C)

D)

24. **Which writing pad represents 3 tens 8 ones - 1 ten 2 ones?**

A) 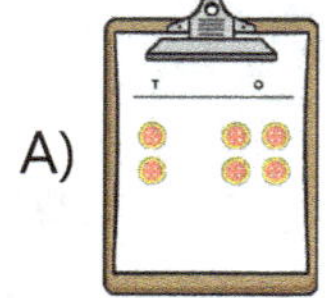   B) 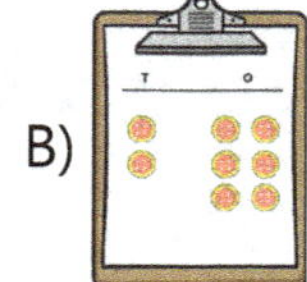   C) 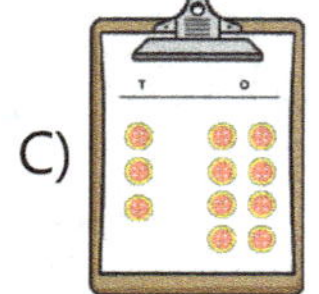   D) 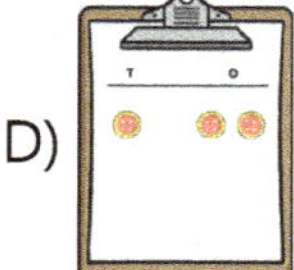

25. Replace P and Q with appropriate signs respectively.

$$9 \ (P) \ 2 = 3 \ (Q) \ 4$$

A) +,-   B) -,-   C) -,+   D) +,+

<table>
<tr><td colspan="5" align="center">Colour your choice with color pencil</td></tr>
<tr><td>1</td><td>2</td><td>3</td><td>4</td><td>5</td></tr>
<tr><td>A B C D</td><td>A B C D</td><td>A B C D</td><td>A B C D</td><td>A B C D</td></tr>
<tr><td>6</td><td>7</td><td>8</td><td>9</td><td>10</td></tr>
<tr><td>A B C D</td><td>A B C D</td><td>A B C D</td><td>A B C D</td><td>A B C D</td></tr>
<tr><td>11</td><td>12</td><td>13</td><td>14</td><td>15</td></tr>
<tr><td>A B C D</td><td>A B C D</td><td>A B C D</td><td>A B C D</td><td>A B C D</td></tr>
<tr><td>16</td><td>17</td><td>18</td><td>19</td><td>20</td></tr>
<tr><td>A B C D</td><td>A B C D</td><td>A B C D</td><td>A B C D</td><td>A B C D</td></tr>
<tr><td>21</td><td>22</td><td>23</td><td>24</td><td>25</td></tr>
<tr><td>A B C D</td><td>A B C D</td><td>A B C D</td><td>A B C D</td><td>A B C D</td></tr>
</table>

CHAPTER 4

LENGTHS, WEIGHTS AND COMPARISONS

TOPICS COVERED:

* Comparing lengths and weights.
* Measuring lengths using: span, feet, unit, a palm, a pace
* Measuring weight using weight scale and length using meter or measuring tape
* Identification of tallest, shortest, farther, nearer, thicker, thinner, heaviest, lightest, bigger, smaller.
* Measuring distance between two objects.

MATHEMATICAL REASONING

1. **Which pencil has the smallest length?**

   A) P

   B) S

   C) R

   D) Q

2. **Which of the following bottles holds the maximum quantity of water?**

   A) 19 Litres B) 15 Litres C) 21 Litres D) 18 Litres

3. **Which of the following is thicker than a** 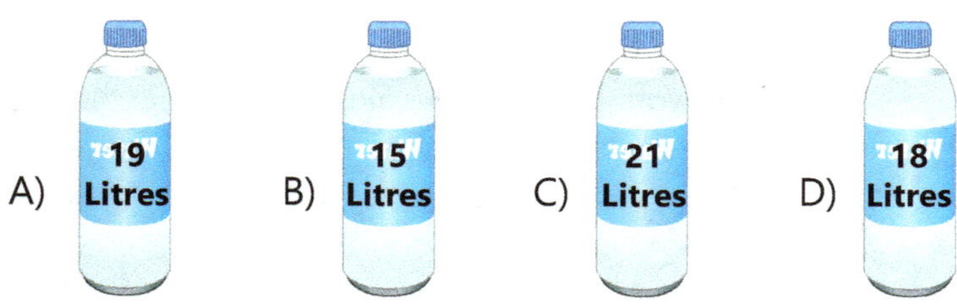

   A)  B) 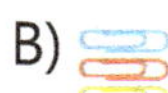 C)  D) 

4. **If each 🥭 stands for 1 unit then the weight of the puppy is _____________ units.**

    A) 14

    B) 12

    C) 18

    D) 9

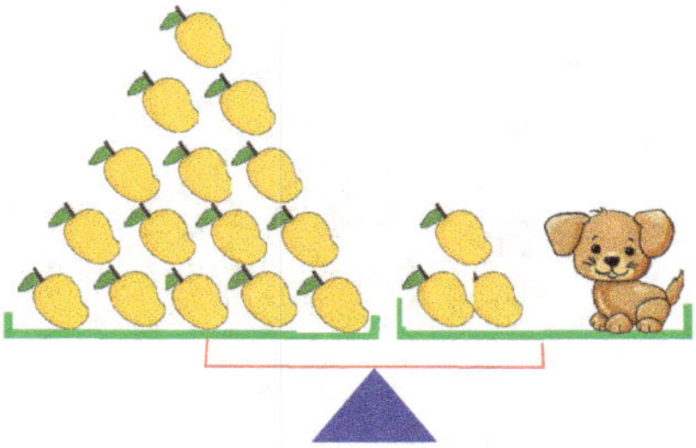

5. **Band ____________ is the longest.**

    A) S

    B) Q

    C) P

    D) R

6. **Distance between two boys is____________.**

    A) 15 Meter

    B) 10 Meter

    C) 20 Meter

    D) 17 Meter

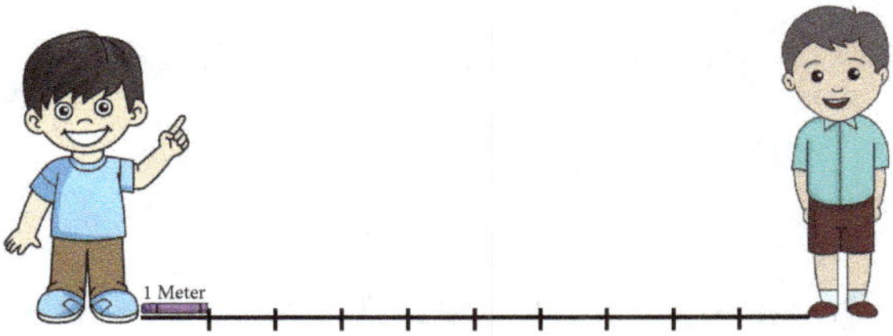

7. **The height of doll is equal to ____________.**

    A) 8

    B) 14

    C) 9

    D) 16

8. **Look at the given garland. Garland _______ is the shortest and garland _______ is the longest respectively.**

    A) R, Q

    B) S, P

    C) R, S

    D) P, R

9. **Match the objects given in column-I with their units of measurements given in column-2.**

Column-1		Column-2
P.	Lenght of wall	1. Kilograms
Q.	Capacity of glass	2. Meters
R.	Weight of rice	3. Liters

A) P-(3) Q-(1) R-(2)

B) P-(1) Q-(2) R-(3)

C) P-(2) Q-(3) R-(1)

D) P-(1) Q-(3) R-(2)

10. **If 1 ～ means 1 unit, then the pen is _____________ units long.**

A) 12   B) 5

C) 9   D) 15

11. **Plate _____________ is the biggest.**

A) P   B) Q

C) R   D) S

12. **Which of the following options shows candies 1 is higher than candies 2?**

A)   B)

C) 

D) None of these

13. **Who is shorter than Giraffe but longer than Tiger?**

A) Zebra   B) Deer   C) Monkey   D) Elephant

14. **Hockey stick is __________ span long.**

A) 7

B) 9

C) 5

D) 10

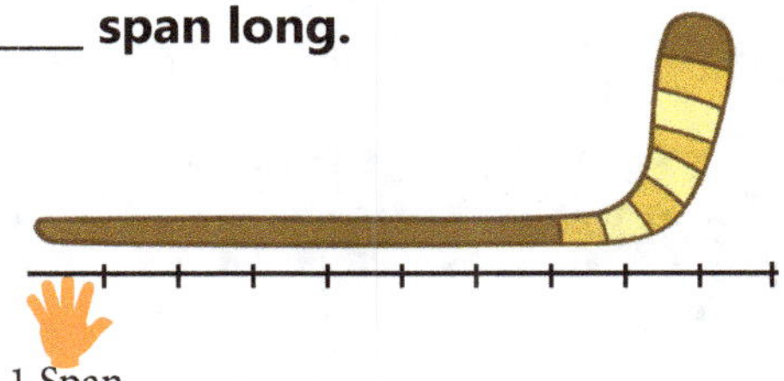

15. **Which of the following is the lightest?**

A)   B)   C)   D)

EVERYDAY MATHEMATICS

16. **Rakesh's weight is 30 kg. Rutuja's weight is 7 kg less than Amar's weight. What is the weight of Rutuja?**

A) 18 kg   B) 20 kg   C) 31 kg   D) 23 kg

17. **Rahul has following two rulers.**   1————— =1 unit

Find the total length of the ruler

A) 8 units   B) 5 units   C) 9 units   D) 6 units

18. **A sugar bag weight is 7 kg. How do 3 such sugar bags weight?**

A) 19 kg   B) 15 kg   C) 21 kg   D) 28 kg

19. **Pranav goes to buy a hockey stick which is 10 cm shorter than his height. His height is 80 cm. What will be the length of the hockey stick?**

A) 80 cm   B) 60 cm   C) 70 cm   D) 50 cm

20. **The Weight of Divya's toy car is equal to 20 marbles. What wil be the weight of two such toy cars?**

A) 30   B) 50   C) 40   D) 60

ACHIEVERS SECTION (HOTS)

21. **Fill in the blanks.**

Writing pad ___________is taller than writing pad R but shorter than writing pad S. Writing pad ___________is nearest to writing pad Q and writing pad ___________is farthest from writing pad P.

A) S, Q, R   B) P, Q, S

C) S, R, Q   D) P, R, S

22. Each 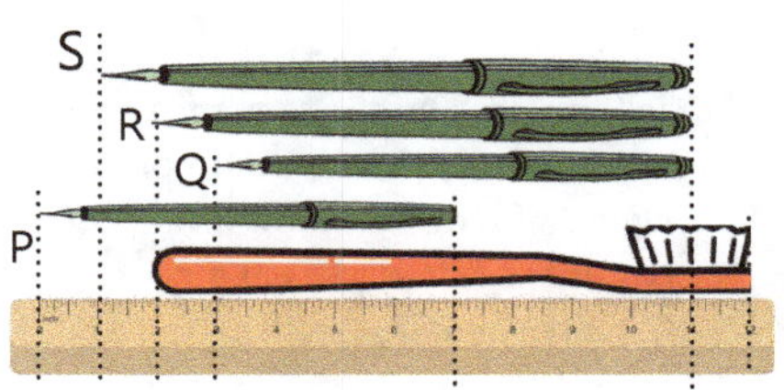 for stands for 1 unit. The weight of is ____units

A) 3 B) 4

C) 6 D) 2

23. Pen ___________is smaller than the toothbrush.

A) S

B) Q

C) R

D) P

24. If a watermelon is also placed on machine A, then which of the following statements is INCORRECT?

A) Weight on machine B is the greatest.

B) Weight on machine A and C are same.

C) Weight on machine A is the least.

D) Weight on machine B is the least.

25. Ashish's height is 85 cm. He needs to reach the total height of 160 cm to reach the top of an wall. The height of which ladder will be most suitable for him?

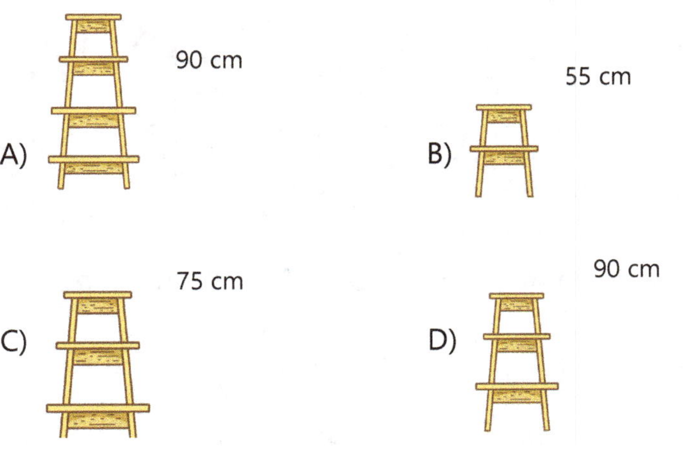

TIME

* Tell the time by the sequence of a day.
* Name of days in a week in order.
* Name of months in a year in order.
* Number of days in each month.
* Calendar reading.

MATHEMATICAL REASONING

1. **You go to play in the ____________.**

   A) Morning   B) Night   C) Evening   D) Afternoon

2. **How many weeks are there in 14 Days?**

   A) 2   B) 4   C) 8   D) 3

3. **If all Sundays are holidays, then in the month of July 20XX how many days we have to work?**

   A) 25

   B) 4

   C) 27

   D) 27

July 20XX						
Mon	Tue	Wed	Thu	Fri	Sat	Sun
			1	2	3	4
5	6	7	8	9	10	11
12	13	14	15	16	17	18
19	20	21	22	23	24	25
26	27	28	29	30	31	

4. **If today is Friday, then day after tommorow will be ____________.**

   A) Tuesday   B) Monday   C) Sunday   D) Friday

5. **In a year, December has ___ days.**

A) 30   B) 29   C) 31   D) 28

6.   Which activity do you do in the night?

A) 

Brushing Teeth

B) 

Going to Bed

C) 

Coming to home from school

D) 

Bathing

7.   How many day of the week is always a holiday in schools?

A) 3   B) 1   C) 4   D) 2

8.   How many months of a year have 31 days?

A) 7   B) 11   C) 12   D) 9

9.   Which is the last month of a year?

A) Febuary   B) October   C) August   D) December

10.   If Dipali's birthday is just after second Sunday of October 20XX, then when will Dipali celebrate her birthday?

A) 10 October

B) 9 October

C) 11 October

D) 12 October

October 20XX						
	Tue	Wed	Thu	Fri	Sat	Sun
				1	2	3
4	5	6	7	8	9	10
11	12	13	14	15	16	17
18	19	20	21	22	23	24
25	26	27	28	29	30	31

11.   ___________comes after March but before July.

A) November   B) February   C) June   D) May

12.   Which of the following months comes just before the third month of a year?

A) February   B) May   C) April   D) July

13.   Which month has 28 or 29 days?

A) March   B) December   C) June   D) February

14. **How many months lie between fourth and seven month of a year?**

A) 7   B) 5   C) 3   D) 2

15. **Which activity do you do in the morning?**

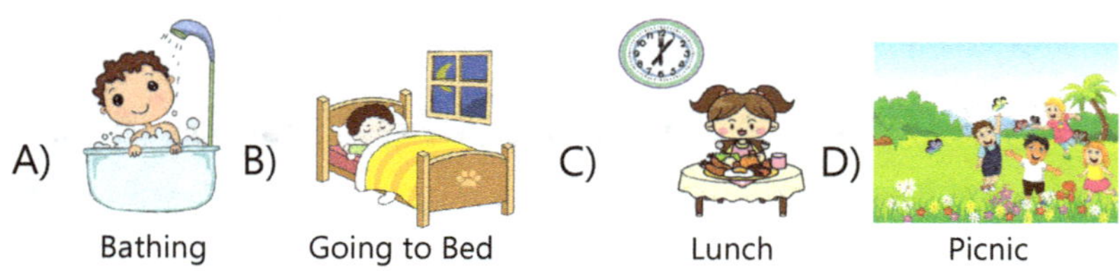

A) Bathing   B) Going to Bed   C) Lunch   D) Picnic

EVERYDAY MATHEMATICS

16. **Which date is just before the second Monday of March 20XX?**

A) March 7

B) March 14

C) March 8

D) March15

March 20XX						
Mon	Tue	Wed	Thu	Fri	Sat	Sun
1	2	3	4	5	6	7
8	9	10	11	12	13	14
15	16	17	18	19	20	21
22	23	24	25	26	27	28
29	30	31				

17. **We go to school after sun rises. It must be ___________.**

A) Night   B) Morning   C) Evening   D) Afternoon

18. **There are___________ days in a year.**

A) 450   B) 365   C) 560   D) 240

19. **Which activity can be done in evening?**

A) Eating lunch   B) Playing football

C) Going to school   D) Sleeping

20. **Which activity do you do in the afternoon?**

A) Wake up   B) Lunch   C) Brushing Teeth   D) Sleeping

21. **If Rishabh's school is reopening on 13th day in the month of June .... 20XX, then on which day will he attend his school?**

A) June 13

B) June 15

C) June 14

D) June 21

June 20XX						
Mon	Tue	Wed	Thu	Fri	Sat	Sun
	1	2	3	4	5	6
7	8	9	10	11	12	13
14	15	16	17	18	19	20
21	22	23	24	25	26	27
28	29	30				

22. **If day after tomorrow is Monday, then 2 day before yesterday was ___________.**

A) Thursday   B) Sunday   C) Saturday   D) Tuesday

23. **Which of the following images shows CORRECT sequence of**

A) Lunch → Sleeping → Picnic → Wake up

B) Wake up → Brushing → Bathing → Going to school

C) Brushing → Bathing → Going to school → Lunch

24. **If a month has 4 weeks, then how many days will be there in that month?**

A) 31   B) 29   C) 30   D) 28

25. **Harshali's vacation started on first Wednesday of March 20XX and lasted for 20 days. Her vacations finished on ____________.**

A) Monday

B) Tuesday

C) Wednesday

D) Sunday

March 20XX						
Mon	Tue	Wed	Thu	Fri	Sat	Sun
1	2	3	4	5	6	7
8	9	10	11	12	13	14
15	16	17	18	19	20	21
22	23	24	25	26	27	28
29	30	31				

Colour your choice with color pencil

1	2	3	4	5
A B C D	A B C D	A B C D	A B C D	A B C D
6	**7**	**8**	**9**	**10**
A B C D	A B C D	A B C D	A B C D	A B C D
11	**12**	**13**	**14**	**15**
A B C D	A B C D	A B C D	A B C D	A B C D
16	**17**	**18**	**19**	**20**
A B C D	A B C D	A B C D	A B C D	A B C D
21	**22**	**23**	**24**	**25**
A B C D	A B C D	A B C D	A B C D	A B C D

CHAPTER 6

MONEY

* Identification of coins and notes.
* Count the money shown.
* Use of money in simple shopping activities.

MATHEMATICAL REASONING

1. **Total of coins here is ____________.**

A) 15 B) 17 C) 20 D) 18

2. **Which one of the following is worth 35 rupees?**

A)   

B)   

C)     

D) 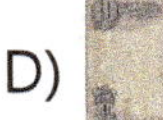    

3. **____is enough to buy this pouch.**

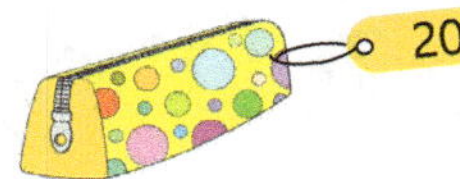

A) 10 B) 17

C) 50   D) 15

4. **Aditi wants to exchange her Rs 50 coins with some notes. Which set of notes can she take?**

5. **How much amount is shown below?**

A) 32   B) 28   C) 35   D) 30

6. **Which of the following costs the less?**

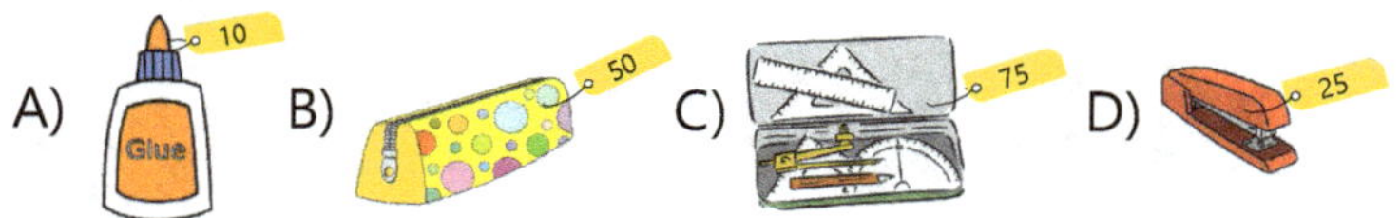

A)   B)   C)   D)

7. **Which amount is more than Rs.80?**

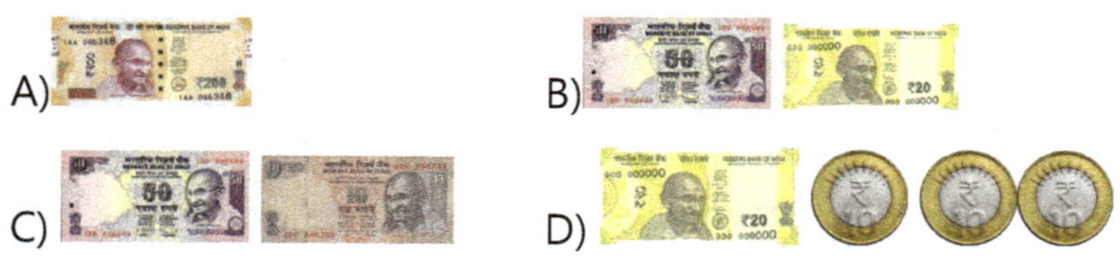

A)   B)

C)   D)

8. **Amount shown here is ______________.**

36

A) 250   B) 200   C) 230   D) 265

9. Vinay pays Rs 150 for  and ___________.

A) 

B) 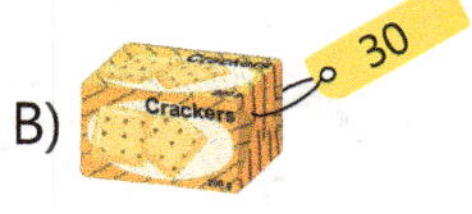

C) 

D) 

10. Sayali wants to buy 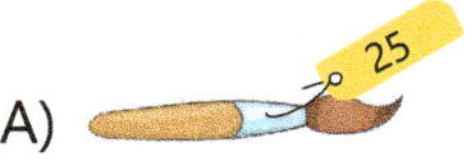 . She has Rs 25. How much more money does she need to buy the toy?

A) 10   B) 15   C) 12   D) 5

DIRECTION (11-12) : Look at the price of each article and answer the following questions.

20	15	5	3	10

11. How much do you have to pay to buy a teddy bear and 2 candies?

A) 12   B)21   C)18   D)20

12. How much do you have to pay to buy three erasers and an ice-cream cone?

A) 25   B) 20   C) 23   D)15

13. Which one of the following amount is the most ?

A)  

B)

C)

D)

14. **How many 10-rupee coins make Rs 100?**

A) 10   B) 20   C) 20   D)100

15. **Which of the following toys cannot be bought from the given amount of money?**

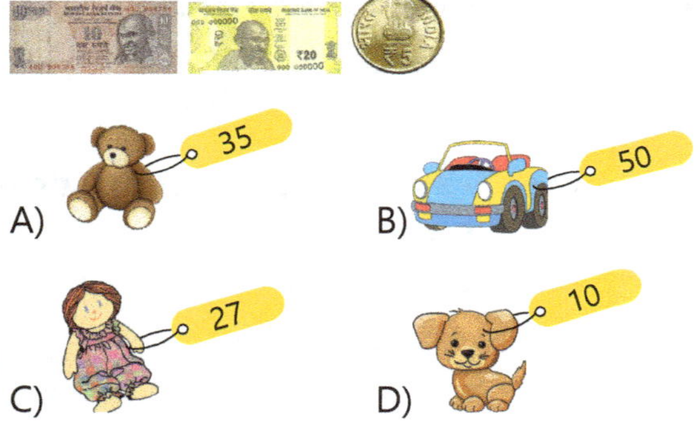

A)   B)

C)   D)

EVERYDAY MATHEMATICS

16. **Rohan has Rs. 15 with him. He gets Rs 10 from Swara and Rs. 10 from Parth. So how much money is with Rohan now?**

A) 35   B) 20   C) 30   D) 40

17. **Divya's Mother gave her Rs 25 as a birthday gift. Which of the following accessories she cannot buy?**

A) 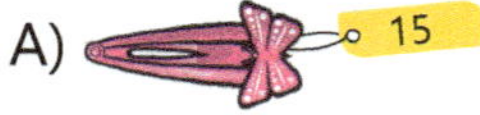

       B) 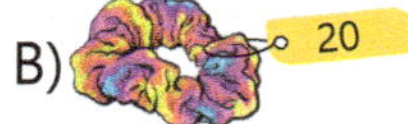

C)  24   D) 28

18. If one ice-cream costs Rs 15, then how much money does Priti needs to pay for 3 ice-creams?

A) 18   B) 20   C) 40   D) 45

19. Vilas gave Rs 30 to shopkeeper to buy the given notebook. How much money will he get back?

A) 20   B) 15

C) 30   D) 10

20. If Manish has Rs 70, then he can buy.

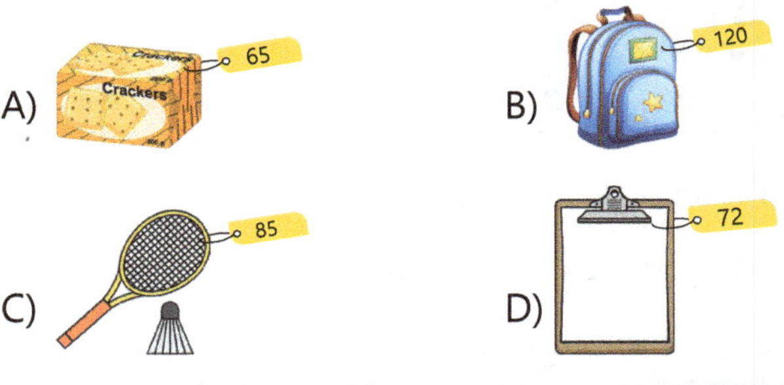

A) 65   B) 120

C) 85   D) 72

ACHIEVERS SECTION (HOTS)

21. Ram wants to buy a 🏏 a ✏️, and an 🍦. After shopping, no money is left with him, how much money he spent?

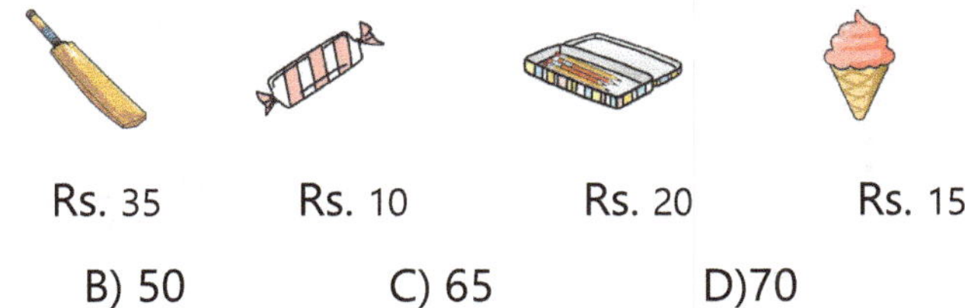

Rs. 35   Rs. 10   Rs. 20   Rs. 15

A) 80   B) 50   C) 65   D) 70

22. Which of the following sets with more number of notes will make up, Rs 90?

A) 4 ten-rupee notes and 1 fifty-rupee note.

B) 1 twenty-rupee note, 6 ten-rupee note and 2 five-rupee note.

C) 4 twenty-rupee notes and 1 ten-rupee note.

D) 1 fifty-rupee note, 3 ten-rupee notes.

23. A schoolbag costs Rs 50. How many numbers of school bags Ankita can buy for Rs 220.

A) 5   B) 8   C) 4   D)1

24. Study the following currency notes and select the CORRECT statement.

A) Rs 500 is the smallest currency note.

B) Total amount shown here is Rs 550.

C) Rs 50 is the biggest currency note.

D) Rs 20 is the smallest currency note.

25. Raj has Rs 110. He wants to purchase three similar items. Which item he can purchase from this store, so that Rs 20 are left with him.

A) Pen   B) Pencil

C) Eraser   D) Sharpener

CHAPTER 7 GEOMETRICAL SHAPES

TOPICS COVERED:

* Identify the shapes and search by their names and drawings.
* Properties of shapes 'rolling, sliding'.
* Identify the solid objects used to draw a shape.
* Identify the shape to be used in the formation of a solid.
* Counting the shapes and solids in a figure.

MATHEMATICAL REASONING

1. The name of shape which is red coloured is __________.

A) Circle B) Triangle

C) Square D) Rectangle

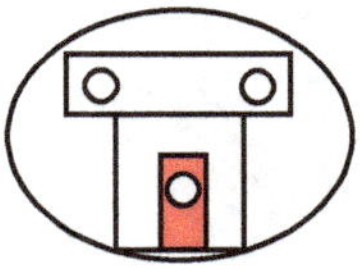

2 There are __________ more triangles than circles.

A) 3 B) 6

C) 2 D) 4

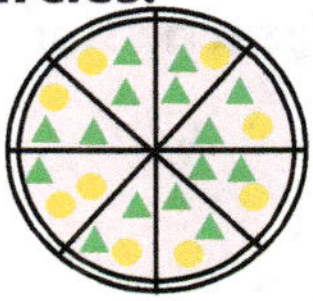

3. Arrange the given plates from the smallest to the biggest.

A) R, P, S, Q B) Q,S, P, R

C) S, P, R, Q D) Q, R, S, P

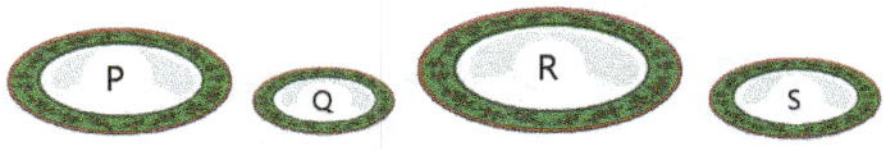

4. Total number of rectangles in the given figure is__________.

A) 5 B) 10

C) 9 D) 5

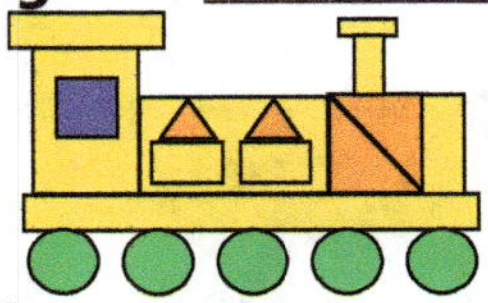

5. A triangle has __________ number of sides.

A) 4   B) 2   C) 0   D) 3

6. ___________ shape is a square.

A)   B)    C) 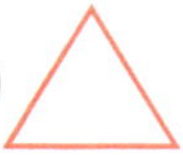   D)

7. The figure is made up of how many squares?

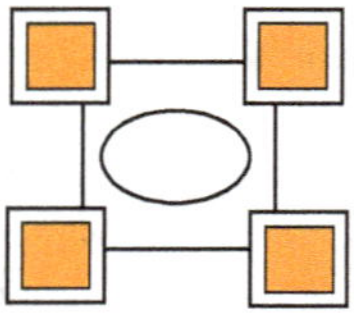

A) 5   B) 9

C) 4   D) 6

8.  can be traced using___________.

A)    B)    C)    D)

9. Which of the following looks like a cone?

A)    B)    C)    D)

10. Which shape is shown here?

A) Circle   B) Sphere

C) Cylinder   D) Cone

11. Name the shape which is yellow coloured.

A) Rectangle   B) Circle   C) Squre   D) Triangle

12. ___________is below the table.

A)    B)

C)    D) 

13. ___________ looks like a cuboid.

A)    B)    C)    D) 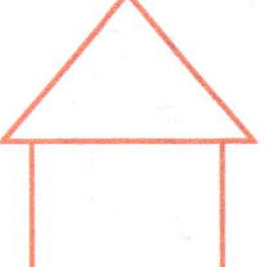

14. Which of the following objects can slide.

A)  B) 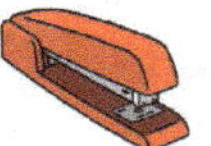   C)    D) 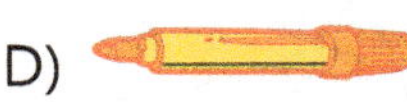

15. Which shapes make up this home?

A) Square,Triangle   B) Circle,Rectangle

C) cylinder,Square   D) cone,Oval

EVERYDAY MATHEMATICS

16. _________ objects are in the box.

A) 1   B) 3

C) 5   D) 4

17. The shape of the soda can shown in the figure is__________.

A) Circle   B) Rectangle

C) Cylinder   D) Oval

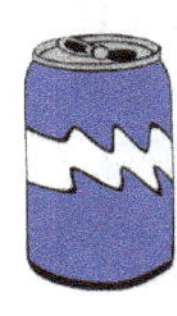

18. Select the CORRECT statement.

A) The shape of a bottle is always rectangular.

B) The boll is always sqare shaped.

C) A book shape is always circle.

D) Compass box is always rectangular shape.

19. **There are 3 squares, 1 triangle and 5 rectangles in Radha's drawing. Which of the following could be Radha's drawing?**

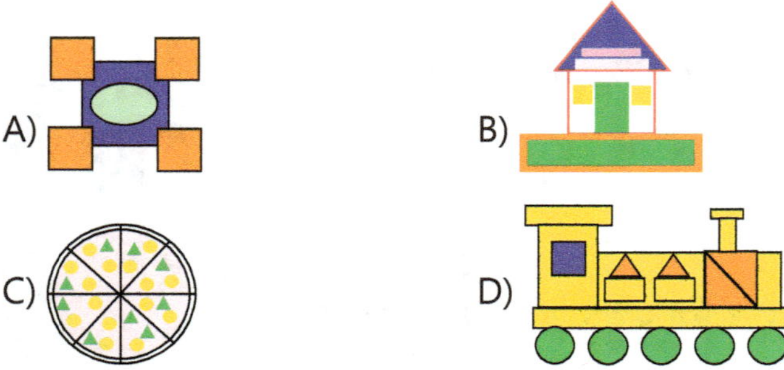

A)   B)

C)   D)

20. **Om has 3 groups of shapes.**

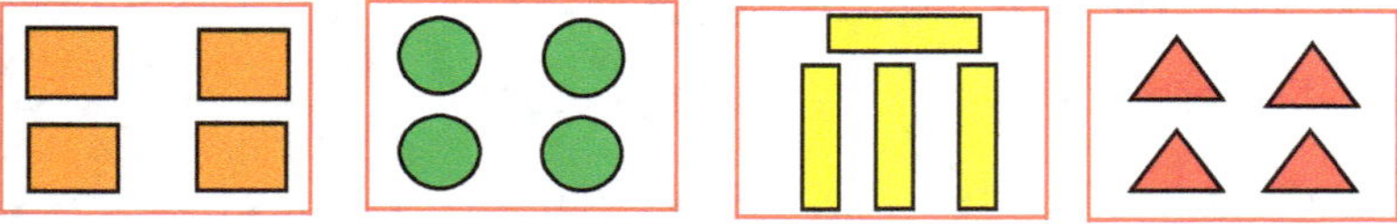

In which group will he put a chalk?

A) Q   B) R   C) S   D) P

ACHIEVERS SECTION (HOTS)

21. **Total number of circles and triangles in the pizza slices are _________.**

A) 16   B) 14

C) 19   D) 11

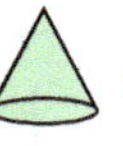

22. **In which of the following groups the shape  can be added?**

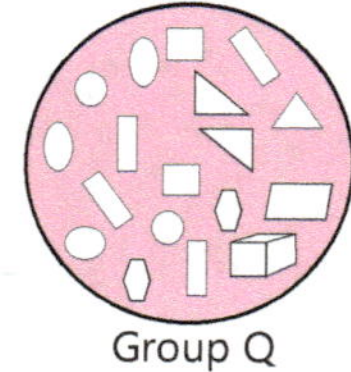

Group P

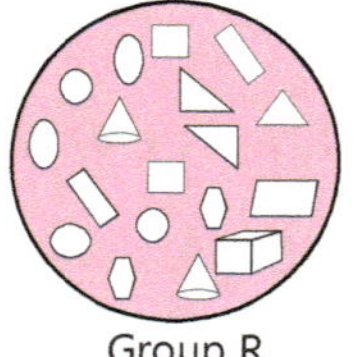

Group Q

Group R

Group S

A) Group R   B) Group S   C) Group Q   D) Group S

23. Select the INCORRECT match of the shape.

A) 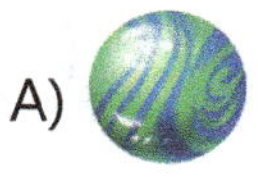

B) 

C) 

D) 

24. There are ________ circles and________ triangles in the given figure.

A) 24, 21   B) 18, 32

C) 27, 15   D) 14, 23

25. Match the shapes in column-I with their names in column-2.

Column 1

P) 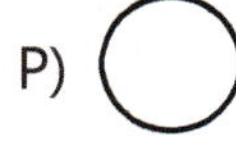

Q)

R)

S)

Column 2

(1)   Square

(2)   Triangle

(3)   Circle

(4)   Rectangle

(A) (P) → (2), (Q)→ (4), (R) → (3), (S) → (1)

(B) (P)→ (1), (Q)→ (3). (R)→ (4), (S)→ (2)

(C) (P) → (3), (Q) → (4). (R)→ (1), (S)→ (2)

(D) (P)→ (3), (Q)→ (1). (R)→ (2), (S)→ (4)

Chapter 8 — LOGICAL REASONING

TOPICS COVERED:

* Number pattern — Next term in the number pattern / Missing term in the number pattern

* Figure pattern — Next figure in the figure pattern / Missing figure in the figure pattern

* Comparison: Inside/outside: Rolling/Sliding: on/under: above/below: top/bottom etc.
* Measuring unit
* Finding the odd term figure
* Identifying the shapes to complete the given figure pattern
* Ranking test: Left/Right/First/Last.
* Analogy: Find the relation between given pair of figures or terms to find the missing figure or term
* Grouping: Making the group of objects. Identifying the group in which the given shape lies

MATHEMATICAL REASONING

1. **Find the next figures in the figure pattern given below.**

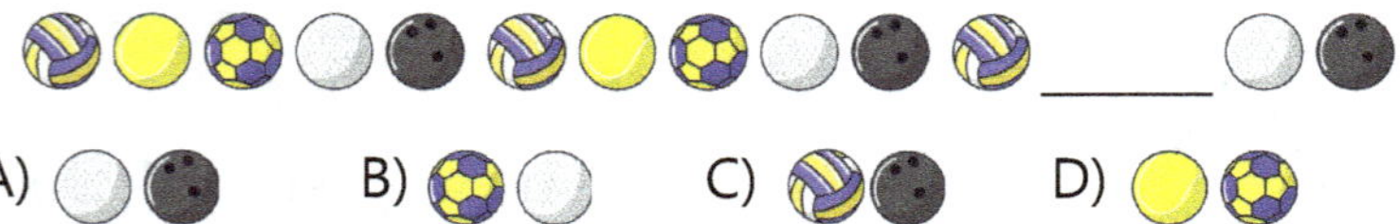

   A)   B)   C)   D)

2. **If Namrata's summer vacation started from second week of May 2OXX, then on which date did Namrata's summer vacation start?**

May 20XX						
Mon	Tue	Wed	Thu	Fri	Sat	Sun
1	2	3	4	5	6	7
8	9	10	11	12	13	14
15	16	17	18	19	20	21
22	23	24	25	26	27	28
29	30	31				

   A) 7th May   C) 8th May

   B) 1st May   D) 15th May

3. **4th object from the left end is _____.**

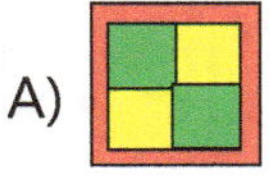
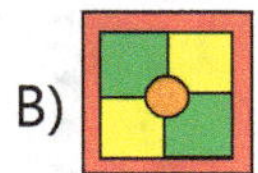

(Left)

A) Square   B) Circle   C) Oval   D) Triangle

4. **Shape made at the top of the figure is____.**

A) Circle   B) Rectangle

C) Square   D) Triangle

5. **Select the figure that is not similar as the given figure.**

A) 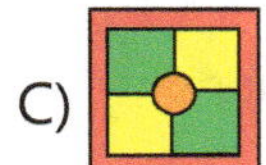   B) 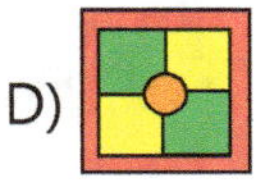

C)   D)

6. **Priya needs _____ rupees to buy accesories.**

A) Rs 10   B) Rs 15

C) Rs 5   D) Rs 20

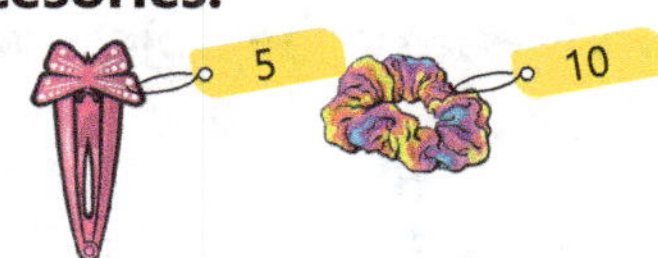

7. **Find the missing figure?**

A) 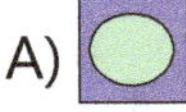   B) 

C) 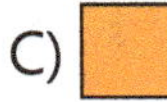   D) 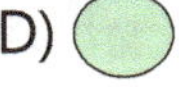

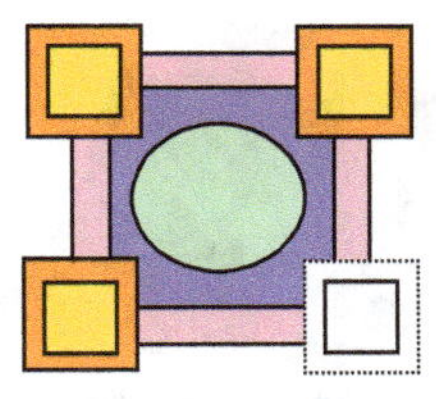

8. **Which number is missing in the given number pattern?**

A) 50   B) 45   C) 40   D) 30

9. **Which shape can be put together with shape S to make a**

square?

A) 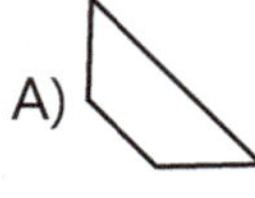

B) 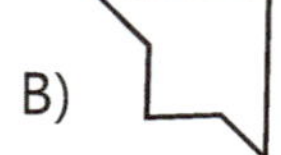

C) 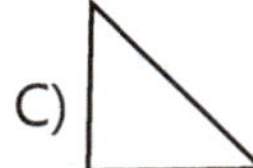

D) 

Shape S

10. **Zebra is standing between _______ and Elephant.**

Giraffe   Tiger   Zebra   Elephant   Monkey   Deer

A) Deer   B) Girrafe   C) Tiger   D) Monkey

11. **Identify the object which is on the table and can also roll.**

A)   B)

C)   D)

12. **Which number comes next in the given number pattern.**

A) 33   B) 20   C) 35   D) 40

13. **How many total number of squares and triangles are there in the given figure?**

   A) 20

   B) 15

   C) 18

   D) 14

14. **____ groups of 2 sharpeners each can be formed from the given sharpeners.**

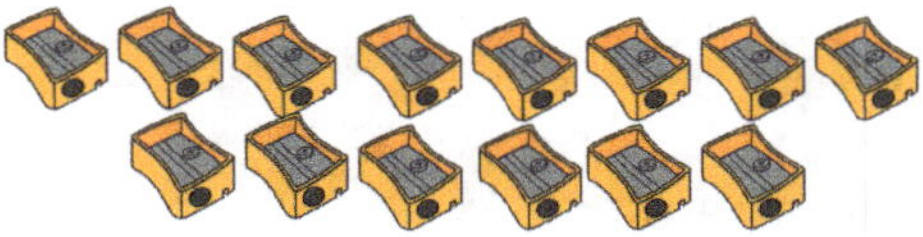

   A) 7   B) 5   C) 6   D) 4

15. **Which fruit is the heaviest?**

   A) R   B) S

   C) Q   D) P

16. **Select the odd object.**

   A) 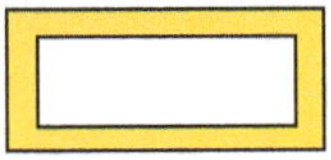   B) 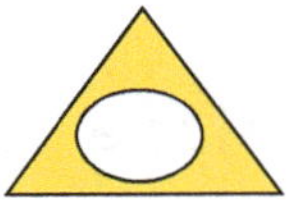   C)    D)

17. **How many fruits are in the the basket?**

   A) 7   B) 8

   C) 6   D) 5

18. **If ▢ is related to ◯ then △ is not related to __**

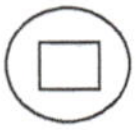

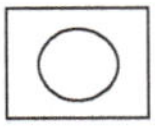

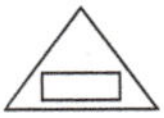

   A)    B)    C) 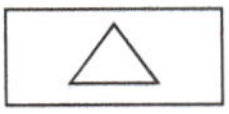   D)

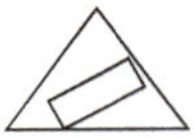

19. **Which crayons is third from the right side in the given**

picture?

A) T   B) R

C) Q   D) S

20. **If today is Friday, then day before yesterday was ____.**

A) Wednesday   B) Saturday C) Thursday   D) Sunday

21. **___ is the biggest pencil and ___ is the smallest pencil.**

A) P, R B) R, S

C) Q, P D) R, P

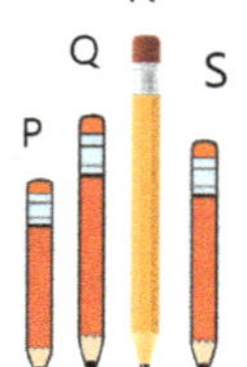

22. **Select the odd one out.**

A) 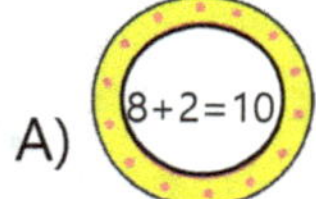
B) 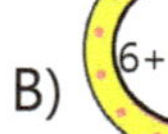
C) 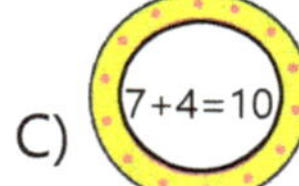
D) 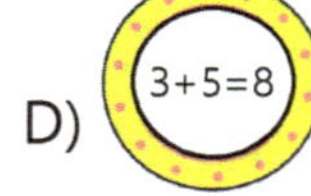

23. **There are __ strawberries outside the plate.**

A) 5   B) 4

C) 6   D) 10

24. **To which object does the shape  belong.**

A)    B)    C) 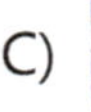   D) 

25. **Identify the relationship of given pair and find the missing figure.**

5 = 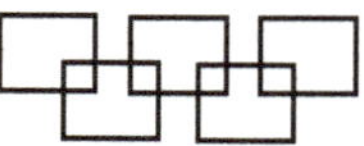   4 = ?

A)    B) 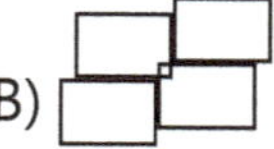   C)    D)

Hints & Explanations

1. (C) : Fifty eight

2. (B) : The expanded form of 78 is 70 + 8 = 78

3. (C) : Scale C shows the smallest number

4. (D) : Sixty five

   Place 5 buttons at ones place and six button at tens place as shown. So, the number comes to be 65.

5. (C) : 34 – Thirty Four

6. (D) : Ascending order is 37, 57,63, 67

7. (B) : Number of oranges 10, Pencil holder B shows 10 pencils

8. (B) :The number which comes before 77 but after 75 is 76

9. (C) : Ninety one is not on the writing pad

10. (D) : 3 tens six ones is 36

11. (B) : The number line represents counting by 3's

12. (C) : Jar (A) has 6 candies,

    Jar (B) has 4 candies,

    Jar (C) has 9 candies,

    and Jar (D) has 2 candies,

    So Jar (C) has highest number of candies

13. (C) : Option (C) shows 8 buttons.

    So option (C) is correct

14. (A) : Option (A) has more objects than the given set of erasers

15. (D) : Thirty four

16. (B) : More than 2 but less the 5 is 4. Basket (B) has 4 apples

17. (C) : Monica has 4 erasers and 3 sharpners.

    So sharpners are not equal to erasers.

18. (B) : 5 Butterflies

19. (B) : 9 Carrots

20. (C) : Rahul has maximum number of candies

21. (D) : Option D has 20 jelly beans.

    So, option (D) is correct

22. (B) : Cone (P) is before cone Q. Cone (T) is after the cone S. Cone R is in (between) the cone Q and the cone S. Cone S is (before) the cone T.

23. (D) : Descending order is S, P, R, Q.

24. (D) : Flight of lady bug by 2's

25. (C) : Number 26 comes before 27.

    So writing pad which shows

2 buttons at ones place and 6 buttons at tens place is the answer.

Hence option (C) shows the number 26

2 Addition

1. (D) : R, Q, S, P
2. (A) : 52 + 13 = 65
3. (B) : 20 + 8 = 28
4. (C) : 3 tens + 2 ones = 32
5. (A) : Number of pencils in pencil box P = 6.

   Number of pencils in pencil box Q = 4.

   Total number of pencils = 6 + 4 = 10
6. (D) : 32 + 34 = 66
7. (B) : Smallest numbers are 9 and 12.

   Required sum = 9 + 12 = 21.
8. (A) : 5th Point
9. (C) : 21 + 3 = 24
10. (B) : 42 + 34 = 76
11. (B) : 11 + 4 = 15.

    So, the missing number is 11
12. (B) : Number of buttons in set Y = 12.

    Number of buttons in set X = 10.

    Total number of buttons in Set Y and set Z = 12 + 10 = 21
13. (A) : Number of buttons in set X = 16.

    Number of buttons in set Z = 10.

    Total number of buttons in Set X and set Z = 16 + 10 = 26
14. (C) : 65 + 10 = 75
15. (D) : (A) 42 + 26 = 68

    (B) 48 + 20 = 68

    (C) 35 + 30 = 65

    (D) 25 + 22 = 47.

    47 is smaller than 65.

    Hence option (D) is correct.
16. (D) : 21 insects
17. (C) : 23 + 6 = 29 Candies
18. (A) : 12 + 22 = 34 insects
19. (B) : 6 + 4 = 10 birds
20. (C) : 15 + 8 + 25 = 48 chocolates.
21. (D) : Each received 4 chocolates.
22. (A) : 1 1 + 2 4 = 3 5
23. (B) : 5 more than 10 is, 10 + 5 = 15
24. (B) : 2 tens + 3 ones = 23
25. (B) : No of ladoos Suresh has = 2

    No of gulab jamuns Suresh has = 5 + 2 = 7

    No of jalebis Suresh has = 2 + 7 = 9

    So, total no of sweets Suresh has 2 + 7 + 9 = 18

3 Substraction

1. (C) : Number line shows 10-4 = 6

2. (B) : Number of bananas 20. Number of bananas crossed 6

   So option (B) is 20-6 = 14

3. (A) : 4 tens 5 ones = 45

   2 tens 2 ones = 22

   So 45 – 22 = 23

4. (D) : Writing pad D shows 28-10 = 18

5. (C) : Largest Number = 96

   Smallest number = 18

   So, required difference is 96 – 18 = 78

6. (A) : 4 less than 12 is 12 – 4 = 8

7. (B) : 4 buttons should be crossed.

8. (B) : 98-60 = 38

9. (C) : Total strawberries = 28 = 2 tens 8 ones

   Number of crossed strawberries = 6 = 6 ones

   So 2 tens 8 ones – 6 ones is correct subtraction sentence

10. (D)

11. (B) : 56 – 21 = 35

12. (C)

13. (B) : For subtraction "18-6", 3 candies should be crossed. 3 candies are already crossed

14. (B) : 52-20 = 32

15. (B) : 53 – 22 = 31 So option (B) 48-17 = 31

16. (D) : 45 - 15 = 30

17. (C) : No of cherries = 15.

    No of strawberries = 7

    No of strawberries requires = 15 – 7 = 8.

18. (B) : 6-3 = 3

19. (D) : 15 – 4 = 11

20. (A) : Sonal has 80 sweets.

    So 80 – 15 = 65 – 25 = 40

21. (B) : X = 8 and Y = 7

22. (D)

23. (C) : 20 – 10 = 30

24. (B) : 38 – 12 = 26

25. (C) : 9 – 2 = 3 + 4

    7 = 7 So option C is correct

4 Lengths, Weights and Comparisons

1. (D)

2. (C)

3. (A)

4. (B) : 🐶 – 3 🥭 = 12 unit

5. (B) : Band Q is the longest

6. (B) : 10 Meter

7. (D) : 1 ▬ = 2 ▲

   Therefore height of doll = 7 ▬ = 16 ▲

8. (A) : Garland R is the shortest and Garland Q is the longest

9. (C) : P – (2) Q – (3) R – (1)

10. (B) : 1 ⌇ = 1 unit. So, length of pen = 5 ⌇ = 5 units

11. (A) : Plate P is the biggest

12. (C) : Option (C) shows candy 1 is higher than candy 2

13. (D) : Elephant is shorter than Giraffe but longer than Tiger

14. (B) : 1 ✋ = 1span. So, the length of hockey stick is = 9 ✋ = 9 span

15. (C)

16. (D) : 30 kg – 7 kg = 23 kg
So, weight of Rutuja is 23 kg

17. (A) : Length of first scale is 3 units and length of second scale is 5 units.
So, total length of both scale is 3 units + 5 units = 8 units.

18. (C) : 21 kg

19. (C) : Height of Pranav = 80cm – 10cm = 70 cm is the length of hockey stick.

20. (C) : Weight of 1 toy car = 20 marbles. So, 20 + 20 = 40 marbles is the weight of 2 toy cars

21. (D) : P, R, S

22. (D) : 2 units

23. (D) : Pen P is smaller than toothbrush

24. (D)

25. (C) Suitable height of ladder = (160 – 85) cm = 75cm

5 Time

1. (C) : We go to play in evening

2. (A) : 2 weeks

3. (D) : We will have to work for 27 days

4. (C) : Day after tomorrow will be Sunday

5. (C) : 31 Days

6. (B) : Going to bed

7. (B) : 1 day

8. (A) : 7 months

9. (D) : December

10. (D) : Second Sunday of October 20XX is 10 October. 11th October is just after 10th October.
So Dipali will celebrate her birthday on 11th October

11. (D) : May

12. (A) : February

13. (D) : February has 28 or 29 days

14. (D) : 2 months

15. (A) : We bath in the morning

16. (A) : March 7

17. (B) : Morning

18. (B) : 365 days

19. (B) : Playing football

20. (B) : Having lunch

21. (C) : June 14

22. (D) : Wednesday

23. (A)

24. (D) : 1 week had 7 days.

28 days = (7+7+7+7) day = 4 weeks.

25. (A) : Monday

6.Money

1. (D) : Amount shown is ₹ 1 + 2 + 10 + 5 = 18

2. (B)

3. (C)

4. (C) : ₹ 20 + 20 + 10 = 50

5. (A) : Amount shown is ₹ 10 + 10 + 5 + 2 + 2 + 1 + 2 = ₹ 32

6. (A) : Glue bottle cost the less

7. (A) : ₹ 200 is more than ₹ 80

8. (D) : Amount shown = ₹ 200 + 50 + 10 + 5 = ₹ 265

9. (D) : Vinay Pay = ₹ 150.

    Cost of Geometry box is ₹ 90. Amount left with him = ₹ 150 – ₹ 90 = ₹ 60. So he can buy the football.

10. (A) : Cost of doll is ₹ 35. Sayali has ₹ 25. So to buy the doll she needs ₹ 35 - ₹ 25 = ₹ 10

11. (B) : Cost of teddy bear is ₹ 15. Cost of 2 candies = ₹ 3 + ₹ 3 = ₹ 6. So total amount to pay to buy a teddy bear and 2 candies = ₹ 15 + ₹ 6 = ₹ 21

12. (A) : Cost of eraser is ₹ 5. Cost of 3 erasers = ₹ 5 + ₹ 5 + ₹ 5 = ₹ 15. Cost of cone is ₹ 10. So total amount to pay the buy 3 erasers and a cone = ₹ 15 + ₹ 10 = ₹ 25

13. (D)

14. (A)

15. (B) : Given amount of money = ₹ 10 + ₹ 20 + ₹ 5 = ₹ 35.

    So among options Toy car cost ₹ 50. So Toy car cannot be bought from the given amount of money.

16. (A) : Rohan has ₹ 15. From Swara and Parth he gets ₹ 10 + ₹ 10 = ₹ 20.

    So ,amount left with Rohan = ₹ 15 + ₹ 20 = ₹ 35

17. (D) : Divya's mother gave her ₹ 25.

    Hair band cost more than = ₹ 20 She cannot buy the Hair band which cost ₹ 28

18. (D) : Cost of 1 ice-cream is ₹ 15. Hence Priti needs the amount to pay for 3 ice-creams is ₹ 15 + ₹ 15 + ₹ 15 = ₹ 45

19. (B) : Vilas gave ₹ 30 to buy notebook.

    Cost of Notebook is ₹ 15.

    The amount of money he will get back = ₹ 30 - ₹ 15 = ₹ 15.

20. (A) : Amount that Manish have is ₹ 70. So he can buy the items less that ₹ 70

21. (D) : Cost of bat is ₹ 35. Cost of box is ₹ 20. Cost of ice-cream is ₹ 15.

    So, amount spent by Ram is

₹ 35 + ₹ 20 + ₹ 15 = ₹ 70.

22. (B) Option B represents more number of note that will make ₹ 90

23. (C) A school bag costs ₹ 50. Amount of money Ankita have ₹ 220. ₹ 220 = ₹ 50 + ₹ 50 + ₹ 50 + ₹ 50 + ₹ 20 = ₹ 220. So Ankita can buy maximum of 4 school bags from ₹ 220

24. (D)

25. (A) Total amount Raj has is ₹ 110. Cost of 1 pen ₹ 30.

So cost of 3 pens is ₹ 30 + ₹ 30 + ₹ 30 = ₹ 90.

So Raj can purchase 3 pens so that ₹ 20 are left with him.

7 Geometrical Shapes

1. (D) : Rectangle
2. (B) : There are 6 more triangles than circles
3. (B) : Q, S, P, R
4. (C) : There are 9 rectangles
5. (D) : 3 sides
6. (A)
7. (B) : The figure is made up of 9 squares
8. (C) : Triangle can be traced using set square scale
9. (D) : Party cap looks like a cone
10. (D) : Cylinder
11. (D) : 'Triangle' is coloured yellow
12. (B) : Ball is below the table
13. (C) : Rubric cube looks like a cuboid
14. (B) : can slide only
15. (A) : The home shape is made up of a square and a triangle.
16. (C) : 3 objects are in the box
17. (C) : cylinder
18. (D) : Compass box is always rectangular shape
19. (B) : Option B has 3 squares, 1 triangle and 5 rectangles. So, figure in option B could be Radha's drawing
20. (B) : Since the shape of the chalk is rectangle in shape. So, Om will put the chalk in group R
21. (D) : Total number of circles and triangles in the pizza slices are 11.
22. (C) : Group Q
23. (C)
24. (D) : There are 14 circles and 23 triangles
25. (C) : P – 3, Q – 4, R – 1, S – 2

8 Logical Reasoning

1. (D)
2. (C) : Second week starts from 8th May.

So, Namrata's summer vacation starts on 8th May

3. (B) : Triangle

4. (D) : Shape made at the top of the figure is Triangle

5. (A) : Figure in option A is not similar as the given figure

6. (B) : The accessories cost ₹ 5 + ₹ 10 = ₹ 15.

    So, priya needs ₹ 15.

7. (B) :

8. (B) : The pattern is 25, 35, 45 55, 65, 75, 85

9. (B)

10. (C) : Zebra is standing between Tiger and Elephant

11. (A) :   is on the table and can roll also.

12. (C) : The pattern is 10, 15, 20, 25, 30, 35

13. (D) : There are 6 squares and 8 Triangles. So total number of squares and triangles = 6 + 8 = 14

14. (A) : 7 group of 2 sharpeners each can be formed

15. (B) : Watermelon is the heaviest

16. (B)

17. (B)

18. (A)

19. (D) : S is third from the right side

20. (A) : Wednesday

21. (D) : R is the biggest pencil and P is the smallest pencil

22. (C) : Except option C sum of numbers in other options is correct.

23. (B) : There are 4 strawberries outside the plate

24. (C) : The shape   belong to

25. (B)

9 788119 373727